GW00502262

Leather on Willow

The Pocket Book of Cricket

Nick Atkinson

summersdale

Summersdale Publishers Ltd
46 West Street
Chichester
West Sussex
PO19 1RP
UK

www.summersdale.com

Printed and bound in Belgium

ISBN 1 84024 442 9

Disclaimer
Every effort has been made to obtain the necessary permissions with reference to copyright material, both illustrative and quoted; should there be any omissions in this respect we apologise and shall be pleased to make the appropriate acknowledgements in any future edition.

To Steph and Jake

Contents

*Anyone foolish
enough to predict the
outcome of this
match is a fool.*

Fred Trueman

Introduction

The game of cricket is the preferred summer pastime of any true gentleman. Quintessentially British in both origin and character, cricket brings together 22 participants, faultlessly turned out in pressed white slacks and beautifully knitted pullovers and split into two groups in a sportingly competitive vis-à-vis battle to score the most runs. Teams the world over slog it out under the sunshine or, in Britain, mostly rain, to prove who can bat the best, bowl the most accurately and catch with the most dexterity. Ironically it began as a game played by shepherds, using a ball made of matted sheep's wool and a wicket-gatepost for stumps and a crooked staff as a bat.

Of course, times change and the modern game differs drastically from its origins. As with most popular sports, cash from advertising has been pumped into the game. Professional players can become rich and aspire to super-stardom. This has brought with it higher levels of competition, skill and supporter expectation, all of which combine to create a far more exciting spectacle today than cricket has previously known.

So, how's your wife and my kids?

Rod Marsh to Ian Botham,
from behind the stumps
during a match

Stumped

The shortest ever Test match was between Sri Lanka and India in Colombo, in 1996. All but 50 minutes of the match was rained out.

Creasing Up

'I can't understand it,' said the captain. 'It was such an important game that I bribed the umpire and yet we still lost.' 'Terrible, isn't it,' a bowler agreed. 'It's getting so you can't trust anyone.'

Simply Not Cricket

In 1944, the **Army** took on the **RAF** at Lord's. Things were progressing smoothly with the RAF batting comfortably, until around 2 p.m., when a familiar noise was heard in the sky. A bomb had found its way into British air space and seemed to be heading straight for **Lord's**. The players did the best they could in such an unexpected situation – they threw themselves to the ground and waited for the impact. Fortunately the bomb missed Lord's by some 200 yards and the game restarted. The batsmen stood up and promptly hit a six off the first ball, restoring the crowd to **cheers**.

Bowled Over

In a Trophy Final in Karachi in 1958
the scorecard read:

1st Innings: Abdul Aziz,
retired hurt, 0

2nd Innings: Abdul Aziz,
did not bat, dead, 0

Batting

Cricket is a reaction sport of the highest order. As well as having a keen eye, good coordination and dexterity, a successful batsman is able to judge the length and spin of the ball from the moment it leaves the bowler's hand and respond accordingly.

Any Brian Lara wannabe needs to consider the correct positioning of the feet, legs, shoulders and elbows, in addition to being aware of the space around him and the whereabouts of the opposition at all times. The batsman must strike a balance between defending his wicket, grabbing runs whenever the opportunity arises and attacking the oncoming ball in such a way that it does not rise off the bat and into the clutches of an awaiting fielder.

The development of cricket into its current state – with higher wickets, flat-edged bats, harder ground and higher ball tensioning – has meant that, in contrast to the 'daisy cutting', ground-trundling bowling styles of the past, the ball is now pitched so that its bounce is higher and closer to the batsman. This has added to the pressure and excitement of the game and batsmen must hone their skills through dedication and hours of practice to ensure victory.

His throw went absolutely nowhere near where it was going.

Richie Bernaud

Stumped

The ball of the century belongs to Australian spinner Shane Warne. His first Test ball in England pitched outside the leg stump and spun across batsman Mike Gatting, taking his off stump.

Creasing Up

The Devils challenged the
Angels to a game of cricket.
'But we've got all the cricketers,'
said the Angels.
'Yes,' exclaimed the Devils. 'But
we've got all the umpires!'

Simply Not Cricket

In the winter of 1878 a team of **cricketers** from Cambridge University challenged a local team to a game on a field just outside the city centre.

Whilst most of the town's **residents** were enjoying the uncommon cold snap by pursuing such classic winter activities as ice skating and curling, the match went ahead on an icy field, with fast **bowling** disallowed and heavily punished. Fielders slid for the ball while the **batsmen** slipped and fell as they attempted to gain any runs. Strangely, the game ended in a very honourable draw.

Bowled Over

C.K. Nayudu hit a ball into
the River Rhea, which is the
boundary between Warwickshire
and Worcestershire, making him
the only batsman to have hit a
cricket ball from one county
to the other.

Bowling

Being able to control the elements of spin, trajectory, pace and accuracy is what makes a good bowler in the modern game. It is an area of cricket that has been utterly transformed since its humble beginnings when it was common for bowlers to 'bowl' the ball along the floor at the pace of an underarm pitch. This was outlawed when a technique known as 'jerking', involving a sharp jerk of the wrist during an under-arm bowl, enabled bowlers to distribute the ball at a pace considered dangerous by authorities.

To enforce this, chalk was applied to the bowler's elbow and if a mark was left on the bowler's trousers, the ball was judged as unfair.

It was this rule of keeping the arm away from the leg that paved the way for 'round-arm' and 'over-arm' bowling as we now see in the modern game.

What's the point in 'O' Levels? They don't help you play cricket!

Ian Botham

Stumped

Surprisingly, the first international cricket match was held between two lesser-known cricketing superpowers, Canada and the USA.

Creasing Up

Ron asked George,
'Tell me, is your daughter's
fiancé a good catch?'
'Good catch?' answered George.
'Dammit, he's the best
fielder we've got!'

Simply Not Cricket

On Wednesday 28 July 1912, Lancashire met Warwickshire at Southport in what was to prove a truly momentous occasion. On Day One, Warwickshire scored 470 on the fourth wicket, a British record at the time. This included **Geoff Humpage** scoring 13 sixes and 24 fours, equalling the British record for sixes. **Alvin Kallicharran** then completed his third double century of the season – breaking another record. On the second day, Warwickshire were forced to make a substitution – bringing on team manager, **David Brown**. Brown then became the first recorded substitute to take a wicket in a match.

Bowled Over

Former Test cricketer Krish Srikkanth added an extra 'k' to his name to make it nine letters long because in numerology, nine is associated with heaven and strength.

Fielding

A fielder's role is to prevent runs being scored with fast returns to the wicket, to catch the batsman out and to stop the ball reaching the boundary. With two players restricted to wicket-keeping and bowling, the remaining nine must alternate between the fielding positions, not all of which are filled at every point during a match. It is the captain's duty to organise his players to fully cover the field.

Coordination, an accurate throw, staying alert over extended periods of play and quick reactions are the main weapons in the fielder's armoury and crucial to any team's chance of winning.

I never play cricket. It requires one to assume such indecent postures.

Oscar Wilde

Stumped

C.B. Fry has not only captained England in cricket but has also represented his country in football, and once equalled the world long-jump record.

Creasing Up

George always played cricket on Sunday. This troubled his wife who asked the vicar, 'Is it a sin for him to play on Sunday?'

'It's not a sin,' replied the vicar. 'The way he plays, it's a *crime*!'

Simply Not Cricket

In December 1967 a game took place in Marlborough College, New Zealand. It was unremarkable except for the performance of 14-year-old Stephen Fleming, who achieved the astonishing result of bowling nine balls in the match and taking a wicket with each one.

Bowled Over

Michael Holding once threw a
ball from the boundary, which hit
one set of stumps and went on to
hit the other set.
Although both batsmen were out
of their creases at the time, the
umpire was too confused to
give either of them out.

Wicket-keeping

Wicket-keepers must be ready for action at all times. It is their job to catch any ball that the batsman misses, to get the batsman out by removing the bails from the stumps with the ball and to receive throws from fielders while the batsmen are running. A wicket-keeper's positioning sense and speed are of paramount importance if he is to do his job successfully.

His position depends on the bowler: for fast bowling, he must stay some distance from the batsman in order to react to edges (when a batsman nicks the ball), while for slow bowling, he can stand closer to the stumps. The more skilled he is, the closer a wicket-keeper can stand to the stumps for fast bowling.

Many a wicket-keeper will testify that diving to catch a ball is not just for the cameras. As well as a moment of cricket glory, it is an essential skill to demonstrate when a batter nicks a ball. A combination of speed and agility can ensure a spectacular catch.

As the player closest to the batsman, the wicket-keeper also strives to throw the batsman off his game with (gentlemanly) comments and quips and often holds the captaincy role because of his unique vantage point. He is the only fielder who can catch the ball with protective equipment, although some maintain that even the padded gloves aren't enough protection.

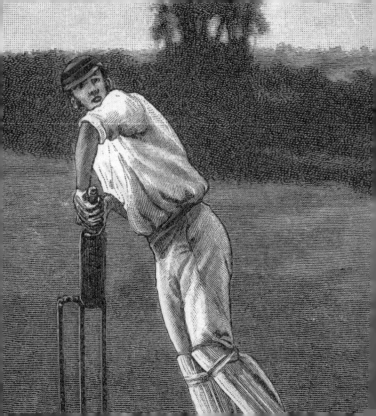

There was a slight interruption there for athletics.

Richie Bernaud,
referring to a streaker at Lord's

Stumped

King of concentration and cricket stamina, Hanif Mohammed once batted for 16 hours and 10 minutes – nearly 3 full days – against the West Indies, scoring 337 runs.

Creasing Up

Two cricketers were talking.
The first one turned to the
second and said, 'So, you had a
hard time explaining the
cricket game to your wife?'
'I certainly did,' replied the
second. 'She found out
I wasn't there.'

Simply Not Cricket

In 1887 at the end of the **Australian** tour, the **English** team decided that rather than face a Combined Australia team, they would divide the teams into **smokers** and **non-smokers**. The game was played out, supplemented by **local Victorian** players and ended in a **draw**, with both teams finishing on 302 for 3.

Bowled Over

Ian Fleming, the creator of Bond, went to the London club Boodle's while he was writing *Thunderball*. He was inspired by the name 'Blofeld' on the membership list and used the name for James Bond's nemesis in the film.

Equipment

The game of cricket uses two bats, two sets of stumps, a ball and a vast array of protective gear.

The bats, which are straight-edged and most commonly made of willow because it is strong and has a slight spring in its structure, vary enormously in size and weight to suit all players. The original 'bat' used by the shepherds was also known as a 'cricce', hence the name of the game.

Cricket balls are made from cork and twine with a leather covering and a stitched seam all the way around the ball. A bowler manipulates this seam to adjust the swing, curve, spin or cut of their delivery.

Cricket players wear a variety of protective gear, which are all stylish yet practical. There are leg pads, chest pads, helmets and gloves for batsmen and wicket-keepers as well as a 'box' for protection of the player's sensitive areas; the balls can come fast and hard!

Let us not forget, however, the ultimate cricketing accessory, the white knit pullover and carefully pressed white slacks – essential for any serious player wanting to really look the part.

The Queen's Park Oval, exactly as the name suggests, absolutely round.

Tony Cozier

Stumped

Strong-armed **Shoaib Akhtar** holds the record for the **fastest ball** in cricket history. The last ball of his second over was recorded at 161.3 km/h (100.2 mph). **Jeff Thompson** of Australia is the proud holder of the record for the fastest ball in Test cricket history. It was clocked at an **astonishing** 160.9 km/h (100 mph).

Creasing Up

How do you recognise an
Australian cricketer at Lord's?

He's the one holding the Ashes.

Simply Not Cricket

In July 1863, a rather strange game of cricket took place. A team of one-legged men took on a team of one-armed men. In a hard-fought contest, the one-legged team won by 21 runs, their hero being a player with no legs, named Letford, who batted tenth and scored ten in the first innings. The *Manchester Daily Examiner* is reported to have assessed his value to the team with the quote, 'Without him, the eleven would not have had a leg to stand on.'

Rules

Although the rules and the strange names used in cricket may sometimes seem incomprehensible to outsiders, all it takes is practice and determination to excel at the game. One way of explaining cricket is as follows: you have two sides, one out in the field and one in to bat. Each man that's in goes out, and when he's out he comes in and the next man goes in until he is out. When they are all out, the side that's been out comes in and the side that's been in goes out and tries to get those coming in, out. Sometimes you get men still in and not out.

When a man goes out to go in, the men who are out try to get him out, and when he is out, he goes in and the next man in goes out and goes in. There are two men called umpires who are both out all the time, and they decide when the men who are in are out. When both sides have been in and all the men have been out, and both sides have been out twice after all the men have been in, including those who are not out, that is the end of the game.

Here are ten ways that a player can get out in cricket...

When a fielder catches the ball before it hits the ground, the batsman is **out caught**. If a bowler catches the ball off their own bowling, the batsman is out caught-and-bowled. If a wicket-keeper catches the ball, the batsman is out caught behind.

If the ball hits the wicket while the batsman is making a run and is outside the crease, he will be **run-out**. It does not matter which batsman initially hit the ball; if a batsman is running towards a wicket and it is hit by the ball, it is he who will be run-out.

If a batsman gets in the way of a fielder who is about to catch the ball, the umpire can call him **out obstructing the field**.

When a bowler hits the wicket and knocks the bails, the batsman is **out bowled**. The batsman can also be out bowled if he deflects the ball onto the wicket in any manner, causing the bails to fall.

If the batsman is outside the crease, whether he is attempting to gain a run or through bad positioning, a wicket-keeper can hit the stumps with the ball and he will be **stumped out**.

When a batter uses his hands to touch the ball, he will be **out for handling the ball**, although he can use his bat, pads and feet to knock the ball away from the stumps.

If the batsman deliberately hits the ball a second time, he will be **out for hitting the ball twice**. He can, however, hit the ball a second time to protect his wicket.

The batsman will be **out for a hit wicket** if he knocks the stumps, causing the bails to fall. It doesn't matter whether it is his bat, his body or his clothing that hits; there is no allowance for clumsiness.

If an umpire believes the ball would have hit the stumps if the batsman's pads hadn't obstructed it, then he can declare the batsman **out leg before wicket**, although the ball must be pitched in line with the stumps for this to count.

After a wicket falls, a new batsman has three minutes in which to get to the crease, after which he will be **timed out**.

I don't know what these fellahs are doing, but whatever they are doing, they're sure doing it well.

Pete Sampras,
watching Lara and Ambrose at Lord's

Stumped

Bhausahib Nimbalkar of India was on 443 runs with one day to go in a first-class match. He was just 9 runs short of the then **world record** of 452, held by Don Bradman. Oddly Nimbalkar was **unable to play** on the final day because he had to go and get **married** and missed out on the record.

Creasing Up

The captain was looking for
new blood for his side, which
was struggling miserably.
'OK,' he said to one new member,
'what are you like at wicket-
keeping?'
'Passable,' said the applicant.
'That's no good,' said the captain,
'we've already got one like that. We
want one that's impassable!'

Simply Not Cricket

In 1904 a **President's Match** took place between the president's team and the local village team in Stroud, England. As soon as the president arrived at the crease to bat, he was called away on **urgent** business. The opposing team, feeling it impolite to get a man out in his **absence**, continued to bowl away from his stumps until his return some three hours later. On his return, the president was pleased to find his side had notched up a **respectable** 72 runs.

Bowled Over

During a match between England
and the West Indies in 1986, a ball
bowled by Malcolm Marshall hit
Mike Gatting in
the face, breaking his nose.
Unfortunately the ball then
dropped onto the wicket, getting
Gatting out for a hit wicket.

Etiquette

The 'long walk' to or from the pavilion can be one of cricket's most sobering journeys. When walking out to the crease, the batsman can suffer trepidation and often faces hostility from opposing supporters. An assured walk out from the pavilion can give the impression of courage and anticipated success and intimidate the opposition, whereas displaying one's nerves may instil confidence of victory in the other side.

It is important also to consider the route back from the crease. An unsuccessful batting spell may cause a batsman to rush swiftly back to the pavilion to contemplate his poor display, whereas a successful batting stint will allow the player to take an elongated stroll, basking in his glory while he does so. This is entirely acceptable, as is stopping en-route to tie and re-tie one's shoelaces in order to enjoy the atmosphere and the applause of the spectators.

One must also be smartly dressed in well-pressed white slacks and pullover because a finely turned out player is a highly confident player. This confidence is felt by fellow team members and illustrates commitment to team identity and cause.

Laird has been brought in to stand in the corner of the circle.

Richie Bernaud

Stumped

The **slowest ever recorded** bowling took place in New Zealand in 1921. A visiting bowler fell down a concealed **manhole** as he began his run up towards the crease. It took rescuers a total of 14 hours to free the man and after **14 hours and 11 minutes**, the unhurt man delivered the first ball of his over.

Creasing Up

Which cricket team plays
while half dressed?

The Vest Indies.

Simply Not Cricket

During an unexceptional Middlesex match in 1934, one Bradfield J. Archer was found to be in attendance. On further examination, however, it was discovered that Archer was dead. A post mortem revealed he had been sitting in the same position for thirty years, undisturbed since before the start of the First World War.

Bowled Over

The **Bodyline tour** of 1932–33 was the most infamous event in cricket and caused a diplomatic row between **Australia and England**. The English team had developed a new tactic to get batsmen out – they bowled at their bodies and placed fielders in short fielding positions backwards of square leg. The balls flew off the edges of the bats, as the batsmen struggled to defend themselves, and were caught by the fielders. Following the tour, rules against **dangerous bowling** were introduced and a restriction was placed on the number of fielders permitted backward of square leg.

Ladies' Cricket

Ladies' cricket has been through many periods of encouragement and rejection to get to its current state of acceptance. The first recorded ladies' match was held in England in 1745, between Bramley and Hambleton, although many believe that ladies were cricketing before this, despite the lack of evidence. Cricketing ladies have always exhibited courage and strong will, as shown by the aftermath of one match, when the ladies involved took it upon themselves to challenge the local men's team to a game, to prove that women and men could compete equally at cricket. Unfortunately, the local constabulary received news of the game and arrested the

17 women involved on a charge of causing an affray.

The first ladies' Test match took place in 1926 between England and Italy. The English women demolished the Italians who ran around the perimeter of the pitch, as in rounders, to score runs.

Richie Bernaud:

What's your favourite animal?

Steve Waugh:

Merv Hughes.

Stumped

Mansoor Ali Khan Pataudi,
despite the handicap of having a glass eye,
became a very fine **batsman** and the
youngest ever Test match captain .

Creasing Up

A batsman passed a man in a white coat on his way back to the pavilion. Turning to the man he said, 'That was never LBW – you need glasses.'

And the man in the white coat smiled and replied, 'So do you, I'm selling ice-cream.'

Simply Not Cricket

On 11 September 1960, a game took place between local pubs the Strawberry Vixen and The Leaf and Feather in the Taunton League. Amazingly, the game took only 13 seconds to be decided and uniquely, not a single ball was bowled. The game took place on a blustery and cold day and neither team wished to play. Both teams declared straight away, the home team winning by simply declaring before than their opposition.

Bowled Over

A batswoman, who was several
months pregnant, tired
while batting during a ladies'
league match in Denmark.
The umpire refused her request
for a runner on the grounds that
the incapacity hadn't occurred
during the course of the match.

www.summersdale.com